Nancy Marguerite's Chopin

Nancy Marguerite's Chopin

a poem by
Anne Markham Bailey

2016
GreenBucket Press
Irondale, AL

Copyright © 2016 by Anne Markham Bailey
ISBN 978-0-692-62336-7

All rights reserved. This book or any portion thereof may not be reproduced or used in any manner whatsoever without the express written permission of the publisher except for the use of brief quotations in a book review or scholarly journal.

First Printing: 2016

Green Bucket Press
2433 1st Ave S
Irondale, AL 35210

www.greenbucketpress.com

*For mother
who gave me poetry*

Part One

In a wood frame house
rented and disdained
she plays the Preludes.
The cicadas mount
a vibrating chorus.
The heat thickens.
The heat settles.

Her fingers dance
like spiders spinning
a web hanging
in the morning
above the keys.

Outside the picture
window
the light
lifts and falls
in the grass
through the leaves
as clouds pass the sun.

Inside the little house
the light
lifts and falls
on the piano
through the Prelude;
Chopin fills the air.

Her fingers
press Chopin
from the keys;
a glistening pattern
shadows the room
after sunrise,
after dressing,
after breakfast,
after father and sister
and brother
leave us alone.

When we are alone
she reaches
for the book
in the bench.
She sits.
She opens the book;
she presses it
with a sweep of her hand.
She bows her head,
her hands on her thighs.
She inhales,
lifts her wrists.
Her fingers are long.
She sets them on the keys;
she begins.

She rocks and sways
on the bench.
Her feet lift and fall.
Her arms lift and fall.
Her eyes are dark almonds
following shapes
in a thick book
with a yellow cover.

I am a little girl
beside her.
I feel her hip.
I am newly emerged,
my wings still folded
and wet.
My feet dangle
above the floor.
I do not move from
the bench.
She wraps me.
She releases Chopin
like webbing;
I am loosely fixed,
my wings untried,
thickly separate,
twisted in the space
between sound.

I do not struggle.
I am eyes.
I am ears.
I am a record of the past.

Fast forward
if you will
to a yellow house in
a Southern suburb.
Fast forward
to a young woman
home for the holidays.

The piano is gone;
the house is full of silence.
The light lifts and falls
in the grass
and in the house.
There is no more space;
no space for Chopin,
no space for webs,
no space for the past
or the sound of "Why?"

Part Two

The lady keeps her secrets close
and will not speak.
Her voice cuts her belly,
bulging with stories
she dares not tell.

The past is the past,
she likes to say.
There's no sense
dwelling on it.
You can't change the past.
No sense opening old wounds.
If wishes were horses, beggars would ride.
You can't have it both ways.
The past is better forgotten.

I've said it myself,
echoing
her syntax,
her intonation,
her phrasing,
sealing the past
in silence.

We are leaky containers
full of entrances
and exits,
full of holes

and waste disposal systems.
The past leaks out of us.
It sneaks out of us
like smelly gas.
The past fills entire rooms,
cities,
superhighways
and theme parks.
In a red balloon pumped full,
the skin tight
and thin,
our stories fill the sky,
and the sun shines from behind their spread,
and the moon glows red.

Balloons are leaky containers.
The past escapes.
The tight red balloon droops;
its walls pucker and collapse.

The past splatters on the heads of shoppers
and boys squatted on street curbs,
on the windshields of a million drivers
talking into cell phones.
It plops on the medical student
and the welder.

Once out of the balloon,
the past is heavy and thick,
dense and slick,
like mucilage, hockers
falling from heaven.

When it hits the windshield
of Nancy Marguerite's car,
she looks up.
The red balloon dangles
wrinkled and limp
in an empty sky.
She looks at the thick glob
on the clean glass.
She sees her mother
reeling drunk;
she sees herself
in a cardigan,
she carries her books,
considers her assignments,
steps lightly in a full skirt.

She looks again
at the splattered past.
Her mother is crying;
her face is crumpled.
Look at me
she says,

Look at me.
Nancy Marguerite is silent,
watching,
still.
Five decades are passed.

In her car
her heart is tight,
like a balloon skin
pumped full,
or a bra that doesn't fit,
or a toddler wrapped
in webbing.

Nancy Marguerite sits back
in the leather seat,
gripping the wheel.
She closes her eyes.
Louis Armstrong sings;
she listens,
mouths the words.
Mac the Knife slows.
The notes spread into
her heart beating,
ba da dum
ba da dum
ba da dum.
Tears as large as her heart

press her eyelids,
roll down her cheeks,
pearls
soak her dress.
Mama's dead.
Mama's dead.
Mama's dead.

She opens her eyes
and turns the control.
Fluid shoots onto
the windshield
and the metal bars
fitted with blades
remove the past,
remove the splatter.
First to the left,
then to the right,
the thick past is pushed
onto the hood
and slips off
into the street
into the gutter
into the rush of waste
that runs underground.

I cross the street
in front of her.

I hear the music
and I watch
behind a lamp post
like a gangster.
I smell
burnt potatoes and fish,
scotch on her mother's breath.
I see
gold light
escaping the car doors,
red light outlining too,
Satchmo singing
Mother's blood.
I am deafened by the heartbeat.

Oh, cold and alone.
Oh, red rubber uterus
flabby in the sky.

I stand behind the post
my arms wrapped tight
around myself
newly born,
newly snatched
from the heartbeat,
from the Prelude.

Darkness drapes the scene
and a spotlight comes up
on the car.
The fluid squirts up
and the wipers come on.
Nancy Marguerite wipes her mother away.
She slices the webbing.

The past is the past,
she likes to say.
I leave my post and
jump in the gutter.
I stomp like a toddler.
I am wet.
I am a fledging.
I unfold my wings
patterned with stories.
The past is present between us.

Part Three

Oh Mother,
the space between notes
rings clear.
Silence swings;
a hanging bridge
links one sound to another.

You leap the bridge,
do not want your weight
to press the planks of memory,
the neat snap of the past
behind you,
before you
in a great wave,
do not want
to dangle above
the great river
with nothing but ghosts
to support you.

I lie on the floor
the length of a day
and listen to the Preludes,
diving for almond eyes
in the towering kelp,
in the waving light,
round eyed fish lifting and falling,
graceful hands

lifting and falling,
a wood framed house
settling on the bottom's tilt.

I stand up.
The great river roars,
tosses spray like pearls,
like stories
catching in webs,
balanced
like Chopin.

Colophon

This single poem was written over a period of years and is risen from the childhood of the poet and her relationship with her mother, crafted in the solitude and longing of the Chopin Preludes that her mother played regularly in the wooden rental house in Vestavia, Alabama in the mid 1960's.

About the Poet

Anne Markham Bailey holds an MFA in Book Arts, an MA in Creative Writing and is the author of "Cold Stone, White Lily." She has been published in numerous journals and literary magazines, and her work was featured at The Watson Library in the Metropolitan Museum of Art. She is a creative writing teacher and collaborates with writers and musicians in a variety of performance venues including The Birmingham Museum of Art and The Birmingham Civil Rights Museum.

annemarkhambailey.com

Green Bucket Press

Founded in 2016, Green Bucket Press is devoted to projects that support authentic voice. Projects include creative products, book publishing and spoken word/recording projects.

For more information: greenbucketpress.com

www.ingramcontent.com/pod-product-compliance
Lightning Source LLC
Chambersburg PA
CBHW031219090426
42736CB00009B/992